Castles

Sue Graves

Nelson

Contents

Why castles were built	4
The first real castles	6
The motte	6
The bailey	7
Castle building	8
Keeping safe from attack	10
The moat	11
The drawbridge	12
The portcullis	13
Defending the castle	14
The lord's family	16
The lord's wife	16
The lord's daughter	16
The lord's son	18
Servants	20
The turnspit	21
Warwick Castle	22
Glossary	24

Why castles were built

Castles were first built nearly 1,000 years ago. They were built to be the homes of lords.

The lord lived in the castle with his family, his followers and his servants.

The lord and his family, followers and servants

A lord often had a lot of enemies. The enemies wanted to attack the lord and his followers, and steal the castle and the land.

A castle was built to protect a lord and his followers from attack.

A castle protected a lord and his followers

The first real castles

The motte

The first real castles were motte and bailey castles. A motte and bailey castle had a strong fence and a ditch around it to protect it from attack.

A motte and bailey castle

The motte was a mound of earth. There was a wooden watchtower on top of the mound of earth.

The bailey

The bailey was next to the motte. It was like a big courtyard.

There were lots of buildings in the bailey. There was a Great Hall, stables and a chapel.

Castle building

Wooden castles were quick to build.

They were also quick to burn down!

People began to build castles out of stone.

It took many years to build a stone castle.

A stone castle being built

The stones for the castle had to be cut and shaped. Men, called stonemasons, shaped each stone to fit closely in the walls and towers.

Stonemasons at work

Keeping safe from attack

Stone castles were often built in places that were hard to reach. This helped to keep them safe from attack.

A castle built on a hill could not be attacked easily.

Sometimes, a castle was built next to the sea.

The moat

A moat was often built around a castle to keep it safe from attack.

A moat was a wide ditch.

Sometimes, the moat was filled with water.

The drawbridge

The only way to get across a moat was to go over a drawbridge.

drawbridge

Soldiers guarded the drawbridge. They pulled up the drawbridge if anyone attacked the castle.

The portcullis

At the end of the drawbridge, was a strong gate. This gate was called a portcullis.

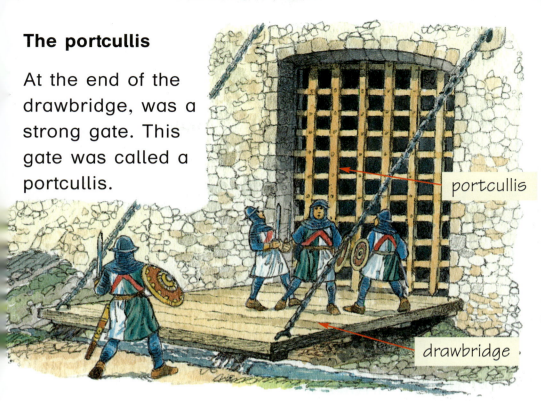

portcullis

drawbridge

During an attack, the portcullis was dropped down.

The portcullis had spikes at the bottom. The spikes could kill an enemy.

spikes

Defending the castle

When the castle was attacked, soldiers lined up along the battlements to defend the castle. The battlements were at the top of the castle walls.

battlements

Soldiers shot arrows at the enemy from the battlements.

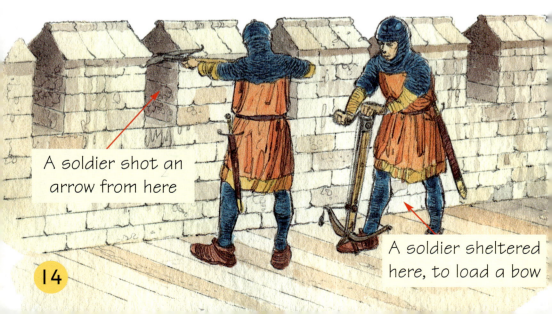

A soldier shot an arrow from here

A soldier sheltered here, to load a bow

There were special holes along the battlements. During an attack, the soldiers dropped horrible things through the special holes on to the enemy.

The soldiers dropped rocks.

They also dropped boiling water.

The lord's family

The lord's wife
The lord's wife looked after the running of the household. She gave orders to the servants to make sure the household was run well.

The lord's daughter
The lord's daughter was sent away from home when she was about six years old. She was sent to live with another lord's family.

She had to learn good manners and to sew well.

It was important for her to learn how to run a household while she was a small girl.

A lord's daughter was married when she was about fourteen.

She could not choose a man to marry. Her mother and father chose a man for her to marry! She had an arranged marriage.

The lord's son

The lord's son was sent away from home when he was about seven years old.
He had to learn to be a knight. The first step was to be a page.

As a page the lord's son had to learn to ride.

He had to learn good manners.

He had to learn to fight.

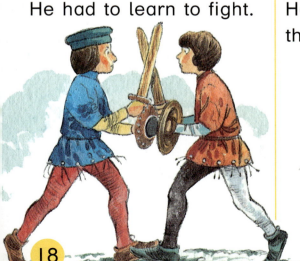

He had to serve food to the lord.

The lord's son was a page until he was fourteen. Then, he was made into a squire. He had to be a squire before he could be a knight.

A squire could be made into a knight when he was twenty-one. A lord had to dub the squire and then slap him hard when he made him a knight.

A lord dubs the squire

Servants

The castle servants worked very hard. Some servants cleaned, and others cooked.

Boys, called scullions, worked in the kitchens. A scullion had to do many different jobs.

He had to clean the cauldrons.

cauldron

A scullion had to get water from the well.

He had to wash the dishes, too.

The turnspit

This scullion was called a turnspit.
A turnspit had to keep turning the big spit with the meat on it.

The meat was roasted over a fire.

A turnspit roasting the meat

Warwick Castle

There are many castles that you can visit today.

Warwick Castle is built on the banks of the River Avon, in Warwickshire.

Warwick Castle is a very old castle. It dates back to 1068 AD. That makes it almost 1,000 years old. You can still see the original motte.

At Warwick Castle, you can see what life was like in medieval times.

You can walk around the battlements, or across the drawbridge.

You can watch a tournament.

A tournament

You can even visit the dungeon. Prisoners were kept in the dungeon of the castle.

The dungeon in Warwick Castle

Glossary

bailey – a large courtyard of a castle

bow – a weapon which is used for shooting arrows

cauldron – a very big cooking pot

chapel – a church

dub – to tap with a sword

knight – a man who wore armour to go into battle. He fought on horseback.

motte – mound of earth which a castle was built on

page – a boy training to become a knight

scullion – a boy who worked in the kitchen

tournament – a contest

turnspit – a boy who turned the meat over the fire